AF245066

OTHER BOOKS BY JOHN BRADLEY

POETRY

Agitprop (2019)
Erotica Atomica (2017)
And Thereby Everything (2015)
Love-In-Idleness: The Poetry of Roberto Zingarello (2015)
One Day You a Mountain Shall Be: The Lost Poetry of Cheng Hui (2014)
You Don't Know What You Don't Know (2010)
Terrestrial Music (2006)
Add Musk Here (2002)
To Dance with Uranium (1995)
The New Wine Dreaming in the Vat (1993)
From the Faraway Nearby (1992)
Love-In-Idleness: The Poetry of Roberto Zingarello (1989)
All for Blanca (1988)
A-E-I-O-U (1981)

PROSE

Trancelumination (2011)
War on Words (2006)

ANTHOLOGIES

Eating the Pure Light: Homage to Thomas McGrath (2009)
Learning to Glow: A Nuclear Reader (2000)
Atomic Ghost: Poets Respond to the Nuclear Age (1995)

EVERYTHING IN MOTION, EVERYTHING AT REST:

A Gallery of Photo-Poems

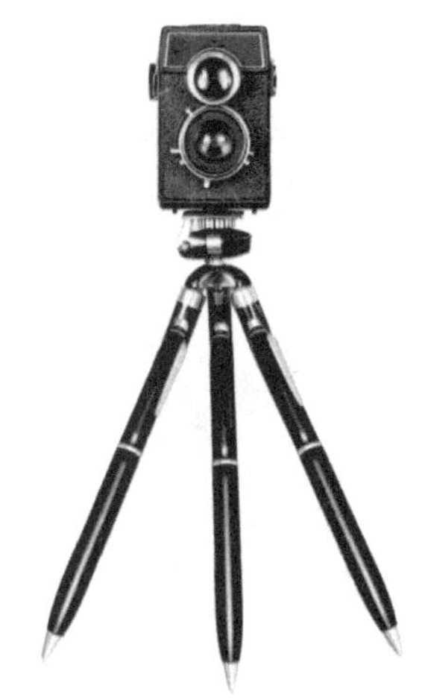

JOHN BRADLEY

DOS MADRES

2020

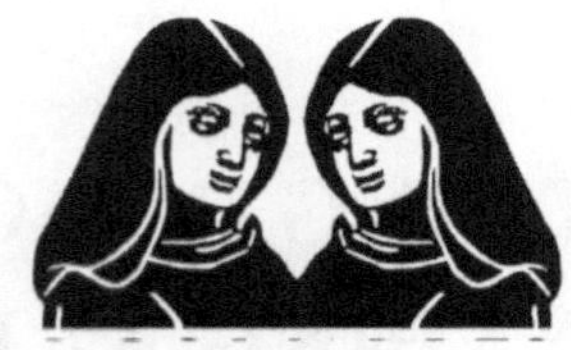

DOS MADRES PRESS INC.
P.O.Box 294, Loveland, Ohio 45140
www.dosmadres.com   editor@dosmadres.com

Dos Madres is dedicated to the belief that the small press is essential to the vitality of contemporary literature as a carrier of the new voice, as well as the older, sometimes forgotten voices of the past. And in an ever more virtual world, to the creation of fine books pleasing to the eye and hand.

Dos Madres is named in honor of Vera Murphy and Libbie Hughes, the "Dos Madres" whose contributions have made this press possible.

Dos Madres Press, Inc. is an Ohio Not For Profit Corporation and a 501 (c) (3) qualified public charity. Contributions are tax deductible.

Executive Editor: Robert J. Murphy

Illustration & Book Design: Elizabeth H. Murphy
www.illusionstudios.net

Typeset in Adobe Garamond Pro & Warnock Pro
ISBN 978-1-948017-72-5
Library of Congress Control Number: 2019956323

First Edition
Copyright 2020 John Bradley

Published by Dos Madres Press, Inc.

ACKNOWLEDGEMENTS

Hayden's Ferry Review: "*Siamese Twins*, Rio de Janeiro, Brazil, 1907, Marc Ferrez"

Kerf: "*Boy Reading to Elephant*, Mexico City, Mexico, 2008, Gregory Colbert" and "*Pile of American Bison Skulls Waiting to be Ground into Fertilizer*, Circa 1892"

Lake Effect: "*Lee Miller in Adolf Hitler's Bathtub*, Munich, Germany, April 30, 1945, David Scherman" and "*Motel Manager Pouring Acid in the Water When Black People Swam in His Pool*, June 18, 1964, St. Augustine, Florida, Horace Cort"

Visiting Bob: Poems Inspired by the Life and Work of Bob Dylan, New Rivers Press: "*Bob Dylan at the Typewriter, The Minnesota Daily*, University of Minnesota, Minneapolis, Minnesota, 1959"

Thanks to Bonnie and Ric Amesquita, Marilyn Cleland, Joe and Jean Gastiger, George Kalamaras, Ken Letko, Becky Parfitt, Susan and Christopher Porterfield. And as always, thanks to Jana, who I can never thank enough.

In memory of Susan Sontag
whose *On Photography* planted the seed
for this book long ago

PREFACE

What can you say about a photograph? a photographer once asked me. Where to begin! There's the mysterious art of photographers, transforming motion into still image, transforming light and shadow into composition, which can move us without the use of words. But how much of this art is planned before the camera seizes a moment and how much an instantaneous sizzle of luck and skill (Henri Cartier-Bresson's *Behind the Gare Saint-Lazare*)? Then there's the authenticity of a photograph, image as fact. But is a photo authentic if the photographer posed or arranged the subject in some way (Arthur Rothstein's *Steer Skull*)? Is a photo authentic if the subject was paid (Robert Doisneau's *The Kiss at City Hall*)? Is a photo authentic if the photographer erased or altered something in the photo, something they considered distracting (W. Eugene Smith's *Spanish Wake*)?

Given that a photo can be altered for effect, perhaps we should consider photography not as a truthful recording of a moment, but more a portrayal of an emotional truth. But what are the limits on this type of truth if evidence suggests the photo to be a hoax (Robert Capa's *The Falling Soldier*)? Lastly, are there some photos that should never be taken (Kevin Carter's *Vulture Waiting for a Starving Girl to Die*)? These questions arise again and again in these galleries.

But I also hope the poems celebrate the beauty and complexity of photography, as well as the artistry and dedication of photographers. I wish to thank all the photographers whose images inspired these poems. For those who wish to see the photos, the title of each poem provides the information needed for the reader to track down the photo online.

What can you say about a photograph? Take this simple test. Drop a photo in your mortar; grind it with the pestle. What remains? Nothing—but the dust of words.

TABLE OF CONTENTS

GALLERY ONE

GALLERY FOUR

Photographs lie.
Even great photographs.
Especially great photographs.

—Tom Junod

A picture is the beginning of misstatement
and misunderstanding. You got people looking at it
with all different opinions,
and they make up stories to go with them.

—Wild Bill Hickok
in Pete Dexter's *Deadwood*

GALLERY
ONE

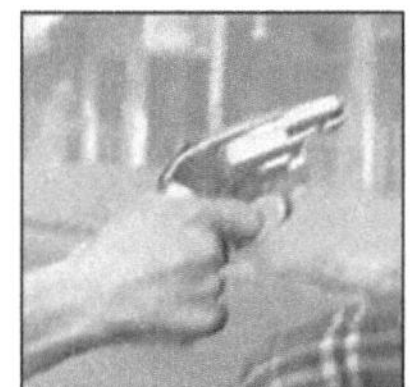

*Saigon Execution (General Nguyen Ngoc Loan
Executes a Viet Cong Prisoner, Nguyen Van Lem),*
Saigon, Vietnam, February 1, 1968, Eddie Adams

Try. Try to look away. The thin, taut arm of Saigon police

chief Nguyen Ngoc Loan. His gun pointed directly at the head

of V.C. suspect Nguyen Van Lem, hands bound behind

his back. The general pulls the trigger of his Smith & Wesson.

Eddie Adams shoots. The prisoner winces. Mouth partially

agape. Bullet churning through his brain. 1/500th of a second.

On a Saigon street during Tet. *These guys kill a lot of our people,*

the general explains. *I think Buddha will forgive me.* No

comment from Nguyen Van Lem. No comment from

Buddha. *The summary execution of an illegal combatant,*

states the Geneva Convention, *is allowable.* After the war:

Les Trois Continents, the general's pizza parlor, in Burke,

Virginia. Not found on his parlor wall: A Pulitzer Prize-

winning photograph of a public execution on a Saigon street,

on February 1, 1968. After the war: *We know who you are.*

Written in a bathroom stall of the general's pizza parlor.

Two people died in that photo, observes Eddie Adams.

The recipient of the bullet and General Nguyen Ngoc Loan.

I killed the general with my camera. 1/500th of a second.

At sixty-seven, the former Saigon police chief dies—

execution by cancer. Eddie Adams sends flowers to the family,

with a note: *I'm sorry. Photographs lie.* Perhaps

Buddha will forgive us all. But try, try to look away.

Retired Man and His Wife at Home in a Nudist Camp One Morning, Mays Landing, New Jersey, 1963, Diane Arbus

Enter, bids the open front door. We unhurriedly view

the generous belly of the man, at ease with himself

in his large armchair. Wearing only loafers, he opens his

legs to let us see—he has nothing to hide. The framed

nude portrait above him reminds us: Clothing is nothing

but a boring convention. The wife, sitting forward

on the sofa, hands tucked in her lap, right foot pulled back,

is not as sure about all this as her husband. She keeps her legs

pressed together, though she lets us see her bare breasts.

On the television, by the lamp and the cat-eyed clock, framed

nude photos of the couple, further evidence, if you need it:

We see the skin as another kind of clothing. In case

you're wondering, Diane Arbus keeps her clothes on while

shooting. She later calls the couple, wanting to pursue more

photos. But the wife refuses to speak to Arbus: *She was sort*

of like an anthropologist collecting specimens. She knew

too much. It made me uncomfortable. Four years after

posing for Arbus in the nude, wife and husband divorce.

Lonely Metropolis, Berlin, Germany, 1932, Herbert Bayer

Two open hands hover before us, both sliced off

at the wrist. They extend from white shirt cuffs, which extend

from the sleeves of a suit jacket. On the building behind,

black velvet shapes mimic the pale fingers. Strapped to the right

wrist, there's the back of a leather watch band, which means

at every moment we'll never know what time it is. All this time,

we've been spied upon. Not from one of the shadowy

windows in the sleepy apartment building. But from those

unsparing eyes in the center of each hand. Could a bored surgeon

have removed these eyes from their former habitation

and transplanted them here, in the palms? Along with the long,

unruly eyebrows? Or did the eyes and eyebrows migrate down

the arms to the soft center of the hands? Perhaps seduced

by their warm, enticing folds, their craven beckoning? Stare

as long as you like, and these eyes, these anonymous eyes

never blink. Even as someone breaths heavily outside

the door. Even as the head—missing the eyes—lies

on a pillow unable to sleep, staring up at the ceiling.

Lee Miller in Adolf Hitler's Bathtub, Munich, Germany,
April 30, 1945, David Scherman

Her eyes turn. Looking at something near the ceiling. Her right

hand pauses on bare left shoulder. About to scrub with Hitler's

washcloth. To wash away the unspeakable. Note how Lee Miller

resembles the small nude sculpture on the side table. The Angel

of History. Right arm raised. Hand resting on her head. Face

turned toward the past. She wants to say: *Awaken thee the dead.*

Make whole what has been smashed. But the words, they clot,

choke. Off to the right, the Fuhrer glowers in his portrait. Hands

on hips, he glares at this intruder in his immaculate bathroom.

Note the two weary army boots on the white throw rug. Stained

with Dachau crematorium ash. Lee muses. Her watch on the chair

ticking. In the Fuhrerbunker, Hitler chose the revolver. Eva

Braun the cyanide capsule. *Promise me,* Hitler told his aide,

you will burn my cadaver, again and again. How soap and water

promise to restore the body. To purify. Washcloth in hand, Lee

waits for the camera. For the world to see this simple act

of vengeance. The heavy boots. The filthy throw rug.

The inflamed Fuhrer. The Angel of History. Shedding her

dirt, here, in Hitler's bathtub. For our viewing pleasure.

Siamese Twins, Rio de Janeiro, Brazil, 1907, Marc Ferrez

I, Dr. Eduardo Chapot Prevost, present for your edification

these Siamese twins, Maria Francisca and Maria de Lourdes,

naked, but for the pink ribbon in the hair, tied by the family

nurse. Joined, as you can see, from chest to stomach,

by a length of tissue measuring eight-and-one-half inches.

This four-legged creature, nevertheless, is one of us, though

the girls possess no navel. You may observe the umbilical

knot at the base of the connective tissue, binding the two

girls like the wings of a silken butterfly unable to fly. The one

on the left, quiet, reflective, will cry at the bark of the softest

voice. The other, on the right, the one with splayed feet, more

talkative, even bold, said, *Doctor, will I be able to skip rope*

by myself after we are broken apart? These children I give

to the faithful camera of Mr. Marc Ferrez, of Rio de Janeiro,

not as an abomination unto your sight, but that they may be

recorded, our trials upon this wanting earth, and how we slowly

learned to disentangle our fleshly flaws. Now if you will

excuse me, I must bid you leave, in preparation for this most

exacting surgery. May the good Lord forgive us all.

Self-Portrait of a Drowned Man, France, October 1840,
Hippolyte Bayard

Observe the swollen face, the swelling hands. Evidence of ongoing
decay. The corpse before you—the late Monsieur Hippolyte Bayard,
unfortunate inventor of the photographic process that brings to you
this fatal image. M. Bayard, unlike Louis Daguerre with his so-called
daguerreotype, fixes the fleeting image directly onto velvet paper.
Bayard unveiled his diaphanous images on March 20, 1839. Daguerre
produced his clumsy copper-plated plates much later, on August 19,
exclaiming: *I have captured the light and arrested its flight!* For this,
nameless French bureaucrats awarded Daguerre honor—and financial
support. Thus the drowned inventor, Bayard's deathless, moldering
corpse. Observe the round straw hat that so became him. The puffy
face, slowly bloating hands. That disturbing smell, ladies and gentlemen,
offending your judicious nostrils, urges us to move on. Could it be
possible that Bayard, to protest his unfair treatment, his unrecognized
genius, staged this self-portrait, faking his tragic demise? Trust your
faithful eyes. Drown yourselves in the unfaltering photographic truth.

The Falling Soldier (Loyalist Militiaman at the Moment of Death), Cerro Muriano, Spain, September 5, 1936, Robert Capa

Everything is always unraveling, says the Falling Soldier, his

right arm letting go. In Cerro Muriano. Or is it Espejo, thirty

miles away? Either way, the dry sky trundles by. *You're stricken,*

says the bullet. *Struck,* says the soldier, casting his rifle away.

Note: Just below the left thigh. Emerging fingers, curling. The art

of letting go. *Nothing is truly beautiful,* says Capa. *Until it ruptures*

through my aperture. Granite sky. Rasping grass. Collapsing

body. But is the famed photo posed? The dead man falling:

For Capa. For his Leica. His *Falling Soldier.* Years later, Capa

is asked: *What if you were presented with a young girl burning*

to death? Capa: *About 1/60 at f5.6.* His fingers curling round

his Leica. Like that day in Spain. The anonymous soldier: Federico

Borrell Garcia. Spanish anarchist. Who died September 5, 1936.

In Cerro Muriano. But some say Borrell posed. Capa shouting:

Look like you're dying! When a sniper's somnolent bullet

made the fake real. Others say Borrell died that day unseen

behind a tree. And looks nothing like the soldier in the photo,

letting go. Note: The low, brooding mountains. Pale, pooling plain. The soldier's location now identified as: Espejo. Where

no bullet was fired that day. *Art never soothes the heart,*

says Capa. Long before he stepped on the mine in Indochina.

How is it, wonders the Falling Soldier, *everything keeps*

whirling, unraveling. Everything, but me.

*Motel Manager Pouring Acid in the Water When
Black People Swam in His Pool,* St. Augustine, Florida,
June 18, 1964, Horace Cort

In sunglasses, sport coat, white shirt, striped tie, Mr. Jimmy Brock,

at the pool's edge, holds a plastic jug by its base, reaching out

so its contents will spill near the face of a swimmer. *Hey, y'all,*

I'm cleaning the pool, he announces to the white and black bodies

below. *Look. He's pouring acid!* someone shouts. A deep moan

rises from a swimmer's dry throat. Someone laughs, tells Brock,

Do it, man. Brock studies the slow uncoiling of the muriatic acid.

How it pauses mid-air, unsure if it wants to spend its venom.

Later Brock will claim he knew all along the acid, diluted in the pool,

could harm no one. Though some of those who swam that day

disagree. *Poor Jimmy. He's a good man,* says a local. *He just did*

a foolish thing. But those folks, they needed them a good, God-awful

scare. Soon Brock will down a daiquiri or two, call his wife, tell her

all about the criminal acts. Whites paying for motel rooms. Sneaking

their black accomplices into the Monson Motor Lodge pool.
    A "Swim-In"

they call it. Well, he showed them what happens in Jimmy Brock's

pool when you violate the law. *The fools, dreaming they could change*

St. Augustine. Then, God forbid, the whole damned world.

Home of a Rebel Sharpshooter, Devil's Den, Gettysburg,
Pennsylvania, July 5, 1863, Alexander Gardner

So the photographer's assistants staggered your unsteady

corpse. Blown here from Talking Rock, Georgia. From

Chickenbone, Mississippi. So they stumble-stepped you

seventy-two yards into this rocky cleft called Devil's Den. Still,

no harm to your unstirred flesh. Soon to be chaff, scuff.

Sidling dust. So they grabbed the wrong rifle off

the battlefield.   Not a sharpshooter's weapon. Set it here

beside you. Just so. Beside your open cartridge box.

So your head was placed upon the slack haversack. Turned

just so to the camera. Your nearby cap looking like it

accidentally totter-tumbled. From Smackover, Arkansas.

From Scratch Ankle, Alabama. Your face smudged

by gunpowder, lit by lichen. So much work does it take

to make a real war photo. Think of it this way, rebel

sharpshooter. The camera embraces you, preserving you

from mouth-sag. Singe, bloat, rupture. From worm-wind,

maggot-swirl.   The camera in cahoots with history.

In cahoots with the flask of rye whiskey in Alexander

Gardner's back pocket. At the rocky armpit called Devil's

Den. That we might, then, begin to gentle you through.

Blind Woman, New York, New York, 1916, Paul Strand

If her right eye narrows to blur. If her left wanders off

to the unforeseeable. If she has no available name.

If she is known as peddler's license #2622. If Paul Strand

pretends to photograph some part of the world before

him. While he gazes at her secretly through a hidden side

lens. If he never asks if she consents, if she dissents,

if she wavers and withdraws. Then the tongue must be

divided into ten parts, and each of those into ten tenths.

If she wears a sign hanging from her neck that shouts

into the mouth: *BLIND.* If she cannot see how many

coins you drop into her enamel cup to buy a newspaper.

If she can't imagine Paul Strand and his camera even if

he peered directly at her face through a true lens for as long

as he could bear. If she would not appear the same

as the blind woman photographed through the hidden lens.

Then you would beg to have your tongue cut into ten smaller

tongues. And each of those ten times smaller. Then and only

then could you claim: *You cannot say more than you can see.*

Billy the Kid and the Regulators Playing Croquet,
Tunstall Ranch, Lincoln County, New Mexico, 1878, Tintype

Is that you, Billy, darling? Striped sweater. Undertaker hat.

Leaning on a croquet mallet. On the high dry plains. Under

snaggled oak. Veinous sun. Can it be you: Mr. William Henry

McCarty, Jr. Henry Antrim. William H. Bonney. The One True

Kid. Could these be the Regulators and friends? Tom Folliard.

Sallie Chisum. Paulita Maxwell. Josiah "Doc" Scurlock.

"Big Jim" French. Antonia Scurlock. Charlie Bowdre and Manuela

Herrera, off to the right, on horseback. But where, darling Billy,

is your dreaded Colt six-shooter? With the legendary twenty-one

notches cut into that all-too-smooth handle? Let's count the accountable:

One wooden schoolhouse. Twenty-one feet and six inches wide. Two

horses. Five men. Six women. Seven children. Many leafless white

oaks. One Billy: The Inevitable, Interminable Kid. Could this really be

you, darling Billy? On John Tunstall's land? For Charlie and Manuela's

wedding? You armed only with croquet mallet. Gun hand at rest.

The other tucked—do-si-do—behind your back. Such a gentleman,

Billy. Waiting for the infinite moment to sink into tintype. Posing

for the one-eyed monster. Infernal machine: Devourer and preserver

of memory and flesh. Dear, disappearing Billy, the Carnivorous Kid.

*Arizona War Worker Writes Her Navy Boyfriend
a Thank You Note for the "Jap" Skull He Sent Her,*
Life Magazine, May 22, 1944, Ralph Crane

Witness: Natalie Nickerson, head resting on left hand, blonde

hair tied back in a frenzy of white lace. She stares tenderly

at the human skull on the table before her. Her sleek fountain

pen, touching the paper, pauses mid-sentence. She's remembering

what her boyfriend said: *This is a good Jap—a dead one*

picked up on the New Guinea beach. She studies the four

teeth stubbornly clinging to the upper jawbone. So clean, so

smooth, her skull. She thanks her handsome Navy lieutenant

and the thirteen of his friends who thoughtfully signed the skull.

I've named the skull Tojo, she writes. *On my bed table, Tojo*

keeps me company at night. Each night I ask Tojo: "Where

be your gibes now? Your gambols? Your songs? Your flashes

of merriment that were wont to set the table on a roar?

Not one now to mock your own grinning?" And each night

Tojo replies: "In you is the presence that will be, when all

the stars are dead." Imagine, she writes, *Tojo talking*

about the end of stars? As if a skull, a Japanese skull—

so smooth, so clean—could hear what you and I can't bear.

Adolf Hitler Rehearsing His Speech in Front of a Mirror, Munich, Germany, 1925, Heinrich Hoffman

One arm pulled back. The other thrust forward. Fingers splayed.

Mouth open. Eyes caught in naked rapture. Or exquisite pain.

Before the mirror, before the rapt crowd, before the camera,

Hitler poses for each phrase of his own speech, spewing

from the phonograph nearby: *The anvil will be beaten. Until*

out of the anvil. Once more. We forge. A German sword!

The light strikes his forehead, his glazed eyes. He can feel the crowd

sway with his every gesture.   *Better an end with horror,*

he urges the surging crowd, *then a horror without end.* Hoffman

faithfully shoots the rehearsal. Later, he shows Hitler the photos.

No, no, no. This is all wrong. You must destroy the negatives,

he tells Hoffman. *You understand?* Hoffman nods. A decade

after the war, Hoffman publishes his memoir: *Hitler Was My Friend.*

With all the photos of Hitler practicing being Hitler. We see Hoffman's

dear friend looking like a bad silent film actor, in love with his own

image. *I should like to put it on record that I have never been able*

to dislike Hitler, writes George Orwell in 1940. *I would certainly*

kill him. Yet I feel no personal animosity. Because there is something

deeply appealing about him. About a man drowning in his mirror.

Detail of Tina Modotti in Diego Rivera Mural,
Chapingo, Mexico, circa 1926, Tina Modotti

What can be simpler than to picture Tina Modotti photographing

Tina Modotti, her double, in Diego Rivera's mural? This woman

with mouth slightly open, hiding from us behind waves of long,

black, oceanic hair. But which Tina Modotti is this behind

the camera? Is she Assunta Adelaide Luigia Modotti Mondini,

born in Udine, Italy? Tina Modotti the Hollywood silent film

actress, starring in *Riding with Death*? Could this be the model

Edward Weston and his camera fell for, first in California

and then Mexico? Or Tina Modotti the people's photographer

who dares us to look at the calm hands of a day laborer

at rest on a shovel handle. The sore hands of a woman

scrubbing laundry on a river rock. No, this must be the Tina

who models for Diego's insatiable murals, but also

documents those murals with her tripod camera. And then

plays for him the insatiable, breathless lover. Could this be

the same Tina Modotti who will toss her Graflex camera into

the Moskova River, in Moscow, saying: *I cannot solve the problem*

of life by losing myself in the problem of art? And the woman

in the mural, is she foretelling the Tina Modotti fighting for breath in the back of a taxi cab, in Mexico City? Mouth open, her long black hair washing over her eyes. Poisoned, perhaps, by a lover who feared she was not his Tina Modotti. But then all these bodies collapse into the Tina Modotti whose gravestone bears these words by Pablo Neruda: *Bees, shadows, fire, snow, silence and foam, / combined with steel and wire and / pollen to make up your firm / and delicate being.* What can be simpler, Tina, then to photograph a figure in a mural, a woman called Tina Modotti?

Valley of the Shadow of Death, Crimea, April 23, 1895, Roger Fenton, and *Valley of the Shadow of Death,* Crimea, April 23, 1895, Roger Fenton

Two photographs. Of a battlefield known as The Valley

of the Shadow of Death. Each photo shows the same road

in the Crimea. Each photo shot the same day. In one:

The sight passed all imagination. You could not walk without

treading of cannonballs in the road. In the other: empty

road. The very same desolate road, but now all the cannonballs

congregate in the ditch. Which, you may ask, came first?

The road with, or the road without? You choose. Measuring

light. Tracking cannonball motion from one photo to

the other. Leaving the Valley, Fenton's assistant, Roger Sparling,

pulls on his silver flask. Fenton writes to his wife: *The sight*

passed all imagination. You could not walk without treading

of cannonballs in the road. But what of the road barren, bereft?

Cannonballs do not move by themselves, says a cannonball.

Fenton oversaw the scattering, claims Susan Sontag. *Less than*

ten minutes after the invention of photography, says Errol Morris,

people realized they could lie with photographs. Or are we too

skeptical? Perhaps first there was barren road. Then soldiers rolled cannonballs onto it for reuse. For collection later.

Shot by Mr. Fenton to document the economy of war.

I picked up a cannonball, writes Fenton. *Put it in the van.*

Hope to make you a present. Of the Valley of the Shadow

of Death. Near Sebastopol. One road. One day, in April,

1895. Two photographs. Posed or unposed. You choose.

GALLERY
TWO

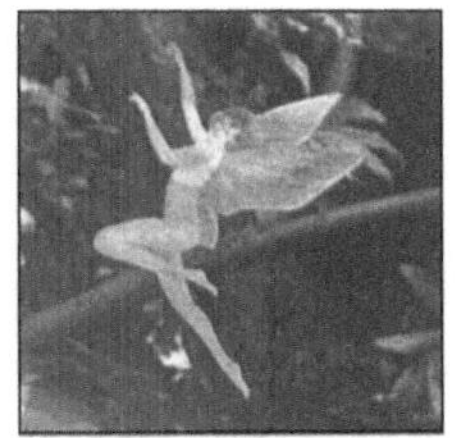

Alice and the Fairies, Cottingley, England, 1917,
Elsie Wright

It all began beside a beck in Cottingley. The two cousins—

Frances, 9, and Elsie, 15—saw fairies flitting by a stream,

and with Elsie's father's camera photographed the impossible.

For the first time ever materialize the fairies at a density

sufficient for their images to be recorded on a photographic

plate, states a Theosophist. In this photo, the first of the five,

Frances, taking on the name of Alice, a garland of flowers

in her hair, stares off into a faraway place where fairies frolic

with humans. Right hand resting lightly on her neck,

she doesn't seem aware of what's bestirring below her chin.

Or perhaps she's fearful gazing directly upon them will frighten

off the winged fairies prancing about, unconcerned

that a camera holds them captive. *This will jolt the 20th century*

mind out of its heavy ruts in the mud, states Sir Arthur Conan Doyle,

who knew all along fairies lurk amongst us, even at 221 B

Baker Street. Decades later, Frances and Elsie finally admit

their fairies are cardboard cutouts held in place with hat pins.

And for those who believe that fairies prance about by beck

and glen, midden and weir? Though she still insists the fairies in the fifth photo, hovering in a bush, are all too real,

says the adult Frances: *You want to be taken in.*

Vulture Waiting for a Starving Girl to Die, Sudan, 1993,
Kevin Carter

Too weak to move, her leaden head bows to the ground. We

witness her furrowed ribs, shrunken arms. Tiny hands. We linger,

we watch, like the vulture. Endlessly patient. Carter shoots

a photo, scares off the vulture. Stumbles about. *I tried to pray.*

I tried to talk to God, he recalls. Unable to erase the vision.

His photo, published in the *New York Times,* disturbs, annoys.

How could he. If the girl. If the vulture. If we didn't know.

Had never seen. Then she wouldn't. We couldn't. Feel this

throbbing in the brain. Carter receives a Pulitzer Prize. Then

late at night irate phone calls. *The man adjusting his lens to take*

just the right frame of her suffering might just as well be

a predator, another vulture on the scene, writes one critic.

Two months after the Pulitzer, Kevin Carter commits suicide.

I am haunted, says the note found by the body. *There are*

always two people in every picture, Ansel Adams reminds

us. *The photographer and the viewer.* Meaning: In every

photograph, there are two vultures. So politely patient.

White Angel Breadline, San Francisco, California, 1933,
Dorothea Lange

Wait. Wait. Wait. In the purgatory called White Angel Jungle.

On Embarcadero and Battery, between Filbert and Greenwich.

Where hands collapse one into the other. Where someone mutters:

This is your country; don't let the big men take it away from you.

Waiting for the White Angel to come, delivering her angelic

bread. Here Dorothea Lange dragged her big, boxy camera. Shot

her first street photograph so we could hear a critic say: *The diagonals*

of the fence posts and the massing of hats do not reduce this work

to the purely formal—the figure in the front middle of the image

acts as a lightning rod for our emotional engagement. In other

words: Hunger an unshaven man in a battered felt hat. Clutching

a tin cup. A dented metal cup weighing more or less than the fluids

in a human stomach. A gelatin silver print, twelve and one fourth inches

by ten and one eighth inches, contains how much hunger? Measured

in length and itch, wait and swell of breadline? *I saw something,*

says Lange. *I encompassed it, and I had it.* And who holds the right

to encompass? To see and possess? *You're not taking anything away*

from anyone: their privacy, their dignity, their wholeness, states Lange.

Or perhaps it's a matter of diagonals. Fence posts. A massing of hats.

On Embarcadero and Battery, between Filbert and Greenwich.

A House on a Hill, Hollywood, California, 1963, Diane Arbus

Cecil B. DeMille. Scarlett O'Hara. Jay Gatsby. Charles
Foster Kane. They must have lived here once. Sipping
vodka and lemonade. Laughing at nothing at all. Now
weeds crackle and hiss. Waver and wait. Above, the clouds
blunder about, white blotches left by a sloppy painter. And behind
the house—Arbus forces us to see—long steel ribs, holding up
the false front. Leave it to Diane to find a house without rooms,
without depth, only the insufferable front. *All signs, all surfaces
reveal us,* raves Arbus the revelator. But look—at the far right
window. A drowsy light. Some insomniac reading *The Day
of the Locust.* No, that's just the sky yawning. Light caught
pretending to be light. *I think it does, a little*, confesses Arbus,
hurt to be photographed. Look at the weeds, how they ache
and heave, swelling to break the dwelling down. The story
goes they found Diane adrift in a bathtub. Unbound from
her blood at the wrist. Didn't anyone think to take a photo
of her? Posing there in the bathtub? We should have listened,
Diane, when you said: *Take pictures of what you fear.* One more
reason, if you need it, to shoot yourself every three minutes.

Jack Ruby Shoots Lee Harvey Oswald, Underground
Police Garage, Dallas, Texas, November 24, 1963, Robert Jackson

Dear Jack. Dear Jackie. Did I shoot that puke Oswald? In the gut?

Like the photo says I did? JFK wasn't anything like me. And for that

I thank the God who gave him to us. And curse the God who
      took him

away. Dear God. Dear Jack. Something's wrong when everything's

so wrong. America is an open wound and they keep tearing more

and more flesh out of the gash. As they keep asking you: *Does it hurt*

now? How much? More? Oswald, he was a Russian handjob,

Cuban stooge, CIA wannabe. Mostly 100% American

fuckup. Sometimes only a handgun can speak for everyone.

Did I shoot that puke Oswald? In the gut? With my middle finger

on the trigger? Like the photo says I did? Dear Jack. Dear America.

All I remember is that pulsing blue light around that clown's body.

Neon blue stripper light. And that sick look on his sick face. The blue

light got brighter. Bluer. I had to shut my eyes. What he did to Jack.

Our Jack. Bits of his brain. Oh God. All over Jackie. And that

cute sonofabitch smirking. Sometimes only a bullet. A .38 Colt

Cobra. Dear America. What else would you have me do.

The Corpse of Ernesto "Che" Guevara, Vallegrand,
Bolivia, October 10, 1967, Freddy Alborta

Don't kill me, I'm Che Guevara! whines the Bolivian colonel. Braying

the alleged last words of the Cuban guerilla. On cue, the soldiers laugh.

Another officer rests his hand on Che's head, as if claiming ownership

of the kill. To show all how obscenely brave the brave military. How

dead the dead Che, on a stretcher, resting on a concrete slab. In the laundry

room of Nuestra Señora de Malta Hospital. They tilt Che's head forward

that we might better view his corpse. As if no one would notice how

the pose resembles Mantegna's *The Dead Christ.* No one would notice

the resemblance to Rembrandt's *The Anatomy Lesson of Professor Tulip.*

Here, says the instructional finger of the Bolivian colonel. *Death undid*

him. Here. And here. Just before they amputate Che's hands. Immerse

them in formaldehyde. Transport them to Buenos Aires. To confirm

the kill. Proof: We exterminated. We rid the world of Ernesto "Che"

Guevara. See: His cadaver on a concrete laundry slab. Displayed for you

to view. At your convenience. *Too beautiful,* says Susan Sontag. *Much*

too beautiful. Thus, she notes: *Like every other, the photo finally fails.*

Napalm Girl, Route One, Outside Trang Bang, South
Vietnam, June 8, 1972, Nick Ut

I'm wondering, mutters Richard Nixon, *if that photo was,
you know, fixed.* No such wondering for nine-year-old Kim
Phouc. *I saw the fire over my* body, she says, remembering
her back. Her left arm. *My clothes just burn off.* After he'd seen
what his camera saw, said Nick Ut: *I don't want no more
pictures.* Which leads us to: *Forgive me*, John Plummer tells
Kim. *For I was the pilot who dropped the bomb.* And then
later: *For I ordered the air strike.* Then later still: *I lied.* Caught up
in emotion. The heat of the photo. He embraces the wounds
he never made. *Too hot,* Kim yells to the god named Napalm.
Eating her clothes. Flesh. Birth-song. *But the camera's cruelty,*
says Susan Sontag. To Richard Nixon. To John Plummer.
To Kim's scars. *Only produces another kind of beauty. My heart
is cleansed,* says Kim to the flame furrowing her flesh. Warning:
Repeated viewing of this photo may cause retinal scarring. Craving
for amnesial water. Artisanal sleep. *The more a photograph
tells you,* Diane Arbus reminds us, *the less you know.*

Behind the Gare Saint-Lazare, Paris, France, 1932,
Henri Cartier-Bresson

Should you believe the critics, Henri Cartier-Bresson, after

jamming your Leica's lens in between the railings of a fence

at the railroad yard, you saw, in the microsecond it took to shoot

this photo: The absurd leap of the rail worker (1) from

the sunken ladder (2) in the flooded railyard just before

his right boot heel (3) kisses the leaping boot heel (4)

in his unearthly reflection on the water. You noted the rings (5)

in the water around the ladder (2) echoing the large metal

hoops (6) in the water, as well as the curve of the artwork (7)

in the poster (8) in the background. You observed the silhouetted

dancer (9) in the poster (8) leaping like our leaping man (1),

only in reverse. You saw the name *RAILOWSY* (10), found

on the poster (8) near the dancer (9). And knew this name (10)

was a pun on your location—the railyard. And a pun on how

the prone wooden ladder (2) in the water resembles rails.

And how RAILOWSKY (10) appears twice on the poster (8),

as if reflected, just like the image of the leaper (1) in the water.

You also recognized that lone figure (11) in the back

of the railyard mirroring the unseen lone figure (12)

in the front, peering through the Leica lens stuck between

fence railings. All this, the critics imply, was planned,

as if a paint-by-unseen-numbers canvas. Could they be

wrong? *Of course,* you say, *it's luck.* Of course, Henri.

Knowing when (3), and where (12) the hunter (12) must

appear with his little black box, ready for luck—

and luck only—to strike down his fleeting prey (1).

The Critic, New York, New York, 1943, Weegee

Maybe it's true. Arthur Usher Fellig, better known as Weegee,
got his nickname from the Ouija board. Because he was always
there, his Speed Graphic camera flashing. As if he knew what
would happen, when, where. As with this photo. Mrs. George
Washington Kavanaugh and Lady Decies. Both bedecked
in diamond tiaras and draped in white furs. They alight from
their purring limo. Just as a drunken woman from the Bowery
shambles toward the socialites. Staring with disgust at their
shameless display of opulence. Perhaps the Ouija board directs
Weegee to go the Metropolitan Opera for the Diamond Jubilee?
Tells him something uncanny will happen there. Be sure
to bring your camera. Or perhaps Weegee sends his assistant,
Louie Liotta, to Sammy's bar. To find a soused patron and steer
her to the Opera. Just as the socialites appear, Louie shoves
the drunken critic forward. *It was like an explosion*, remembers
Louie. *I thought I went blind from the flash exposures.* As
the gracious socialites politely smile for Weegee's camera,
unaware of what the exposure exposes. *People are so wonderful,*
says Weegee. *A photographer has only to wait for that
breathless moment to capture what he wants on film.*

Tank Man, Tiananmen Square, Beijing, China, June 5, 1989,
Jeff Widener

No one knows your name, Tank Man. No one knows what

has become of you. Some say after you stood in front

of that row of tanks, armed only with shopping bags, you

were seized by secret police. Then executed. Others

say you were grabbed by civilians, smuggled out of Beijing

to the countryside. Or to Taiwan. That photo—of an ordinary

man in a white shirt and black pants, shopping for leeks

and lapsang souchong, infuriated by the waltz of tanks, tanks

which had rolled over students the day before—is not known

by many Chinese students today. Thanks to the sleepless

internet police, who scrub any trace of protests in Tiananmen

Square that year. To evade the censors, one hacktivist

replaces the tanks with obscenely enormous rubber ducks,

which you bravely, and comically, defy. This image, of course,

also banned. When you see your famous photograph now,

Tank Man, do you look around? Shake your head? Say,

How could a good citizen ever do something so crazy?

Then go on your way, to shop for leeks and black tea.

The Falling Man, New York, New York, September 11, 2001,
9:41 a.m., Richard Drew

There's the Falling Man. Sleek. Anonymous. One leg bent.

Upside down. Surrendering to his fate. And then there's the man

falling—Latino. Goateed. Tall. Thin. In his 30s or 40s. Beneath

his white tunic an orange shirt. A food service worker. At Windows

of the World Restaurant, at the top of the North Tower. Observe

how the Falling Man complements the two towers, verticality

on verticality, note the critics. Thanks to Richard Drew. Who

framed the Falling Man for me and you. Whether we wish

to look upon the Falling Man or not. While the other man,

the man falling, plunges 32 feet per second per second.

Traveling at 150 mph. This man does not fall for me or you.

In these other photos taken by Drew of the man falling, we see

his body in a violent spasm, tossed sideways, arm thrown out.

Photos that went unpublished. Because we prefer to see, don't

we, the Falling Man, not the man falling. *Maybe they're just*

birds, honey, a mother trills to her child that morning bodies

kept falling. Maybe two hundred. Maybe more. Yes, we know

the Falling Man and the man falling are the same man. But

we can't seem to hear one say: *I'm called the Falling Man because*

I'm no longer falling. Because you won't let me finish my fall.

Spanish Wake, Deleitosa, Spain, 1951, W. Eugene Smith

An elderly villager, from another century, lies with hands

crossed over his abdomen. Nearby, wife, daughter, and

granddaughter, along with three other women, mourn

him, in the smoldering gloom of this small room. Only the dead

man's face radiates light, in Generalissimo Franco's Spain.

A true picture, says Eugene Smith, *unposed and real.*

And yet Smith altered this photo. Two of the women,

the dead man's wife and daughter, stared, in the original

photo, into the unrelenting camera. Into our eyes. Asking:

What are you doing here? Smith made another print

with their eyes almost blacked out. Then, with fine-tipped

brush, he added bleach to whiten their eyes, to make one

woman gaze downward, the other off to the side.

His altered photo walling in the mourners with the dead. Walling

us out. A true picture? Unposed and real? *I didn't write the rules,*

says Smith. *Why should I follow them?* Thirty-six years later,

another photographer visits the village, asks about Smith's *Spanish*

Village photos. *Smith enabled our village to be portrayed*

as a collection of backward idiots, states one resident.

As if we were savages! says another. Although

there's now a road in Deleitosa named, yes, Eugene Smith.

36

At the Time of the Louisville Flood, Louisville,
Kentucky, 1937, Margaret Bourke-White

If you haven't already, meet the Whites. *World's highest
standard of living,* hums Mr. White, commandeering the car
wheel. *There's no way like the American Way,* warbles Mrs.
White, gazing bravely somewhere beyond the attainable
future. *Look at me!* blurts Daughter White, beaming in the back
seat, center of the center. *What's that sound I hear thrumming
around my head?* mumbles Sonny White, nervous yet sunny.
*There can be no happiness other than this disembodied
happiness!* barks Lucky White, the pet terrier, his raffish head
sticking out the back window. Somehow none of the Whites
notice the long line of black Louisville residents, flooded out
of their homes, waiting here, at the base of the billboard,
for relief. Some carry shiny buckets. One holds an empty
basket, another an empty canvas sack. Some look dead
into the camera, wondering why we inspect them so. Then
our eyes begin to rise. *No way like the American Way.*

Isadore Greenbaum Dragged Out of Madison Square Garden by Police, New York, New York, February 20, 1939

A young Jewish plumber from Brooklyn. Attending a German-American Bund rally. With over 22,000 arm-raising attendees. Greenbaum wants to know what happens at a *Pro-American Rally.* Wants to hear Fritz Kuhn the *Bundfuhrer.* For three hours, the plumber listens. Then slowly works his way—around the edge of the crowd, past the brown-shirted guards—to the stage. Kuhn calls for a *white, Gentile-ruled United States.* Warns about *Jewish Moscow-directed domination.* George Washington, called *our first American fascist,* looks out over the crowd, regally serene. Unable to bear any more, Greenbaum leaps onto the stage. Shouts: *Down with Hitler!* Then disappears in a swarm of stormtroopers. They beat him. Kick him. Pull down his pants. A brown-shirted boy onstage jumps up and down, gleefully claps. Police pour in. Swarm the interloper. Drag him outside. In the photo, Greenbaum looks seasick, trousers dangling from an ankle. Suspenders looping down to the street. One hand—a detective's? Greenbaum's?—
clutches

his boxer shorts. A bemused cop smiles. Charged with *disturbing the peace,* Greenbaum is fined twenty-five dollars. *People could have gotten hurt*, scolds the judge. Replies Greenbaum: *Plenty of Jewish people might be killed with their persecution.* Footnote: In Germany, Hitler constructs yet another concentration camp.

Ku Klux Klan Members Ride a Ferris Wheel, Cañon
City, Colorado, 1926, Clifton Rolfe

White as white ant, white arsenic, white bean, white beard,
   white-bellied,

white birch, white blood cell, white board, white bread,
   white-breasted,

white-browed, whitecap, White Castle, white cheddar, white
   chocolate,

white Christmas, White Cliffs, white clover, white-comb, white
   corpuscle.

White collar, white dwarf, white elephant, white-eyed, whiteface,
   whitefish,

white flag, white flight, whitefly, white-footed, white fox,
   Whitefriars,

white frost, white gold, white-haired, whitehead, white heat,
   white-heart,

white-hot, White House, white knight, white lead, white lie, white
   light.

White line, white lingo, white list, white-livered, white maggot,
   white

mahogany, white man's burden, white matter, white meat, white
   metal,

white mice, White Mountains, white mulberry, white-napped,
   whiteness,

white night, White Nile, white noise, white-nose, white oak, white
   onion.

White Ops, whiteout, white pages, white paper, white pepper,
   white pine,

white plague, white poplar, white-print, white-quilled, white
     rabbit, white

radish, white race, white rat, white rhino, white room, white
     Russian,

White Sands, white sauce, white slave, whitesmith, white snakeroot.

Whites only, white squall, Whites only, whitetail, Whites only,
     white thorn,

Whites only, Whites only, white-throat, white tie, white trash,
     whitewalls,

white walnut, whitewash, white water, white whale, white wing,
     whitewood,

white wine, whitey tighties, Wite-Out. Belgian white, bobwhite,
     egg white,

Great White, lintwhite, nonwhite: White. 36 Ku Klux Klan
     members,

100% American, in 100% American white robes and hoods,
     on a Ferris

wheel in Cañon City, Colorado; five more by the ticket booth
     posing

with white arms crossed. All peering out—into the spectral future.

GALLERY
THREE

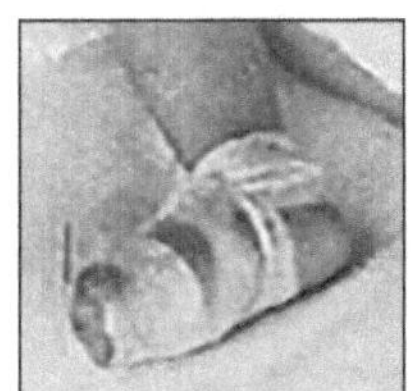

Portrait of a Baby, Hale Country, Alabama, Summer,
1936, Walker Evans

The baby, covered with a square of white linen, sleeps. On

the wooden floor. No cushion, no mattress. Only another piece

of white linen to rest upon. We see a crease down the middle

of the fabric. Someone ironed this. Someone gently wrapped

the baby's injured left foot. The other foot, bare, protrudes past

the white linen bedding. The baby's left hand a fist. A strand

of linen has broken free, on the right, flowing with the woodgrain.

This too is fact. In the dream someone fired wet white towels,

as if from a machine. The open wet towels smacked the human

body hard, like a bomb. Bones snapped. The towel disintegrating

upon impact. But this is no dream. The baby, almost hidden

from sight, sleeps. Upon the floorboards. This the photograph insists.

Like the word of God striking the body. Snapping bone. *It's akin*

to hunting, photography is, says Walker Evans. *In the same way*

that you're using a machine, and you're actually shooting something

and you're shooting to kill. You get the picture you want, that's a kill.

Evans calmly kills the nameless baby. As it sleeps, in the steep

Alabama heat, on the wooden floor. Making a small fist.

Albuquerque, New Mexico, 1958, Garry Winogrand

When you remove this photograph from my mouth. Be careful

not to damage the baby in diapers emerging from the open

mouth of the garage. The tricycle spilled in the sloping

driveway. The rising storm over the rising mountains.

Should you place your finger in my mouth to remove

the photograph. Be careful not to damage the boy behind

the baby, barely visible, lost in garage emptiness. As if unsure

about the intent of the man with the camera. As if waiting

to see how far the baby will go. When you begin to chew

this photograph. Be careful not to damage Garry Winogrand.

He's at the end of the driveway, not sure if he's in Albuquerque

or Rancho Cucamonga. When you swallow this photograph.

When you open your mouth. When words spew out. Be careful

not to say what Winogrand would: *I photograph the world*

to see what the world looks like photographed. All you need

to say is: *Seriously. Who would ever eat a photograph.*

Pile of American Bison Skulls Waiting to be Ground into Fertilizer, Rougeville, Michigan, 1892

I always knew we'd choke, joking about this. How many bison

bones does it take to fill a whiskey glass? 1492. It's true. Crazy

Horse sacked Rome. Buffalo Bill ate Sitting Bull's brain. Depending

on the annual rainfall in Buffalo Chip, South Dakota. Whether you get

two-fifty or fifteen dollars per ton of bones. Note: The dainty derby-

hatted men. One above. One below the bone pile. Dusted with lunar

glow. How a foot must rise and then fall. Upon a propped-up buffalo

skull. To proclaim: *Veni, vidi, vici. I came. I shot. I slayed*

each buffalo I swayed. Note: How not knowing gnaws the known.

The myopic skulls that populate this pyramidic pile. How many?

Depends. On the largess of lethality. What bore. Whether

you slurp coffee or tea. Refine the bones into sugar or fine bone

china. Sullen linen or napkin ring. Pocket watch or whale-bone

girdle. You always knew what you crave. The comfort of a number.

180,000 skulls. All they gave. More. Than always less. What

became of so much offal? Unstrung tongue? *Patience,* sighs

the impacted pile. *One day you too shall fertilize the earth.*

Excusado, Mexico, 1925, Edward Weston

Excuse me, says the camera. *For taking this photograph*
of a toilet somewhere in Mexico. Excuse me for suggesting
a toilet can be a sweeping, ceramic winged Victory
of Samothrace. I excuse you if you don't—*a toilet is*
so mundane, yet so erotic, testifies the camera. For two
weeks, Weston bows before this divine ceramic sculpture
in his motel bathroom. For two weeks, the aching
back. For two weeks: *Contour, contour, contour.*
For two weeks, mumbling: *Human form. Minus*
the imperfections. Only a man who found sensuality
in the undulating folds of a green pepper could say:
It's not what you look at that matters. It's what you see.
Look carefully into the reflection on the toilet, and you
might see, leaning in the doorway, Tina Modotti,
the photographer's lover. *Excusado.* The toilet—
discreet, functional, profane, elegant—observes all,
without judgement. *Just like me,* says the camera.

The Hand, New York, New York, September 11, 2001,
Todd Maisel

There was an unwritten agreement—no photos of 9/11 victims

would be published by any newspaper or shown by any network.

No bloody human carnage. And then, on Liberty Street, Todd

Maisel saw it, there in the gutter, a human hand, forefinger pointing

directly at him. He shot what he found: The yellowing wrist.

White bone shank. Shredded red tissue. Pebbles, cigarette butts,

a small chunk of Hersey's milk chocolate nearby.   He shot

the hand because he held a camera. Because he was a photo-

journalist in New York City on 9/11. Because he'd witnessed

a fire fighter hit and killed by a falling body. Because in his lungs

he breathed the dust of pulverized flesh. He took the photo

because one frayed finger pointed directly at him. Because

the photo says: *This is how it was.* Newspaper editors, network

managers hissed: *Betrayal. Violation.* Viewers of the photo

claimed: *Sacrilege. Lack of decency.* Only this photo lets us see

what we cannot imagine anyone should ever see. Only this photo

of a hand, in the gutter, near a piece of befallen chocolate.

Hunts Point, from *Faces of Addiction*, New York, New York,
May 16, 2015, Chris Arnade

Deserted night on a deserted street. Cinderblock wall on one

side, parked truck on the other. In between, a woman with a grim

face, hands tugging down the top of her dress, to let us view

her breasts. *Got to get $300 by tomorrow,* says the Flickr caption

Arnade provides. As if that explains why this anonymous

woman bares her breasts for Arnade's camera. Did he pay

her to pose? To lean back against a tree and make her plea?

Got to get $300. To advertise the depth of need. To show

the woman's costumer what his or her money could buy. *We use*

each other. I use them for photos, and they use me, says

Arnade, a former Wall Street banker. *Sometimes for $10*

or a ride, and to tell their story, he explains. *Do not pay*

sources or subjects or reward them materially for information

or participation, says one code of photography ethics.

Treat all subject with respect and dignity. Give special

consideration to vulnerable subjects. The photo has 7,681

views. 58 faves. Is it the shamelessness of her pose,

the shape of her breasts that we enjoy? Or the nakedness

of her desperation? Her addiction? *What right,* says Arnade, *do you have to make someone's suffering pretty?* As if

quoting the Gospel of the Gold-Plated Barbed-Wire Spine.

Lange's Foot, 1959, Dorothea Lange

Did your students gasp, Dorothea, when they saw this

photo? Two of your toes bent, angry claws. Did you tell

them how the foot shaped you? How it taught you never

to be a person with a twisted right foot? *Where do I live?*

you had asked them. Answer this question with a photo.

But not with a photo of a street, house, room. Go deeper.

Maybe you read them the poem by Wallace Stevens that opens:

I am what is around me. Some of the students said: *Why don't you*

do your assignment? So you removed your right shoe, raised

the foot polio warped when you were seven, and shot it.

Your only self-portrait. How you loved feet. There's the photo

of a kneeling mother in a shack washing her daughter's foot

in a white enamel bowl. The dirt farmer plowing barefooted.

The close-up of a black sharecropper's weathered bare feet

on a weathered wooden porch, in Hinds County, Mississippi,

a dime on her anklet to ward off headaches. Did the photo

of your foot ward off headaches and foot-aches, Dorothea?

Did it stave off weariness, starve anger? Long before you traveled

along those wind-ravished roads to document the dust-blown,

the undone. You knew: *I live in this body, this vagabond*

body. Look again at the twisted bounty wherein I dwell.

Lewis Powell (Alias Payne), Conspirator, Seated and Manacled, USS Saugus, April 27, 1865, Alexander Gardner

Handsome. Languid. He could be on the Metra. One seat

away. He could be in Starbucks, writing in his Moleskin

journal with his Visconti fountain pen, made from Mount Etna

lava. Filling page after page with one word: *Assassin.*

From the Arabic: *hashshashin. Hashish user.* No one would

guess—this handsome, languid man knifed William Seward,

the Secretary of State, in head and throat. As Seward lay

in his sickbed. The assassin's knife striking metal and canvas—

Seward's neck brace deflecting the blade. Four days later

Powell appears at Mary Surratt's boarding house, on H Street.

Where he's questioned. Manacled. Imprisoned on the *USS Saugus.*

Against riveted steel, he slams his skull. Shouting: *I'm mad!*

I'm mad! Soldiers descend, cocoon his head in a thick, padded

hood. On April 27, Powell consents to pose for Alexander

Gardener's camera. This prisoner named Powell. Or Payne.

Or Wood. Or Hall. Twenty-years old. In wrist irons. He stares

into our eyes. Dares us to call him: *Listless. Languid. Assassin.*

He leans back against the dented iron gun turret. His eyes

taunting us: *War doesn't end because you say it ends.*

Bomb Shelter, Garden City, New York, 1955

It's 7:22 in the shelter. Neither night nor day in the Kidde Kokoon.

Dad, in white shirt and tie, cradles their radio with both hands. His

right ear close to the speaker. *I'm gonna dig myself a hole, move*

*my baby down in the ground. You know when I come up, there
     won't be*

no wars around, sings Arthur "Big Boy" Crudup. Mom, in long skirt

and heels, listens intently. Daughter, next to mom, protects her

black kitten from the scary song with both arms. Nearby, we see

two wooden crates labelled: CANNED FOOD and CANNED
     WATER.

So the shelterees will always know which is which. Near the clock,

which still reads 7:22, we see a flashlight; General Electric Radiation

Monitor; bag of noncombatant gas masks, large; and four books.
     Hard

bound, in case of turbulence. Stacked beside an army shovel: bland

cans of spam, Nestle's Sweet Milk Cocoa, and a boxed cook stove.

No sign of a commode. No problem: *Make your commode by cutting*

the seat out of a chair. Placing the pail under it, instructs the bomb

shelter pamphlet. Two wheels of a toy can be seen behind the
     CANNED

FOOD crate. The Walter Kidde Nuclear Lab providing the nuclear

family with everything they could possibly need in their Kidde
    Kokoon.

Thanks to the radio, Dad, Mom, and Daughter will know when to

emerge from their shelter, will know: *There won't be no wars around.*

Bob Dylan at the Typewriter, *The Minnesota Daily,*
University of Minnesota, Minneapolis, Minnesota, 1959

Who's that skinny kid. Bob. Poking. Prodding. Cig in hand.

Ashy keys. Typing: *This machine fights fascism. But not so good.*

As Lead Belly's guitar. Or. Woody Guthrie. Was born. With twelve

fingers. And a long. Prehensile tail. Or. Oh Betty. Black Betty.

Where can I find. In Dinkytown. Your bam-da-lam. Or. What say,

Hank Williams. We ride the rails. Fore winter. Comes prowlin'

round. Ride that tumbleweed boxcar snake oil dance hall juke joint

moonshine levee revival tent. Not one U. of M. quarter do you last.

Not nearly enough. Universe. In the university. Now the Ten O'Clock

Scholar. Field Holler High. That was school. For a young rounder.

Oh Betty. Black Betty. Let's hop a freight. Bound for Woody.

Bam-da-lam. Typing by day the new name. *Robert Presley.*

Bob Holly. Bobby Lee Lewis. And then. One night: *Bob Dillon.*

Dodge City poet. Sheriff Matt Dillon's bastard son. Born

of tumbleweed lawman backwood dance hall juke joint iron ore

outlaw revival tent. Now you're called *another Barry Manilow.*

By some young skinny punk at the *Minnesota Daily.* The newspaper

where you once poked typewriter keys. Sing it, Leadbelly: *Bam-da-lam.*

Mohammed Ali Meets the Beatles, Fifth Street Gym,
Miami Beach, Florida, February 18, 1964, Harry Benson

In the ring, a young Ali—then Cassius Clay—extends his muscled

right arm. We witness the blow, so long and slow, travel through

George's head, who years later will swear he was in Twickenham

at the time. Through Ringo, who wonders: *Are we still on The Ed*

Sullivan Show? Through John, who knows Sonny Liston will KO

this fool: *The Big, Ugly Bear will drop the Loudmouth in round one.*

Oh, the Blow finally unloads. Kisses Paul on the side of the head.

Making him wail like Little Richard when he heard Pat Boone's

"Tutti Fruitti" croon: *A bop-bop. A loo-mop. A lop-bop-bop.*

I'm in the backseat, behind my father, who's at the wheel. I still don't

know what I said to trigger the blow. A right backhand. My father's

gold Citadel ring striking lip and tooth. Sharp splinters pricking my

listless tongue. End of round four. *Cut 'em off!* Ali shouts to his trainer.

Cut off my gloves! I want the world to see. Sonny Liston cheats.

Something on Liston's glove. Now in Ali's stinging eyes. Water—

sponge—water. The trainer shoves his fighter back into the ring.

Ali can see only a blobbish blur. *Stay away from him! Stay away!*

shouts his trainer. But what is that? On the screen, that arterial

shape, long and slow. The *Maddox* radarman stares. Swears.

It's a North Vietnamese torpedo. No. Maybe it's only echo-shadow-blur. He bites his gum. Waits for the blow. *A-wop-bop-a-loo-bop-a-lop-bam-boom.* The giant bends low, grabs Ringo. Who swoons in Ali's massive arms. *Look,* says John, *it's the bloody bride of Frankenstein.* I curse the big, ugly bear. So low and slow, he can't hear. *Forgive him not. For he knows what he has done.* The lanky sonarman on the *Maddox* swears. He can hear something. A burbling, bragging voice. From the far too near future. Taunting. Jeering: *I ain't got no quarrel with them Viet Cong.* Minutes after the four Moptops leave the gym, Ali enjoys a brisk rubdown. Waiting to bite—long, slow—into a fresh papaya. He turns. Says to the *Times* reporter, *Hey, who were those little sissies?* Could it be? Ali doesn't know the Beatles? The reporter winces. Staggering from the blow.

Fire Escape Collapse, Boston, Massachusetts, July 22, 1975,
Stanley Forman

The woman—head first, arms out, already bracing. The child—
right leg leading, arms spread wide—above the woman. Clumps
of plant soil suspended between them. The child's soft, round
belly. The woman's unseen face, obscured behind her left hand.
The iron fire escape, to their right, like topsy-turvy Russian
constructivist panels. *Note the potted plants*, says one caption.
Not wanting us to miss any of the wonderment provided by this
photo. The ages of the two subjects—nineteen and two—drift
away. Return only when the freefalling ends, when we attach
names to the fallen: Tiare Jones. Diana Bryant. *I was shooting
pictures as they were falling*, states Stanley Forman. *Then I
turned away.* The child survives. Her godmother's body breaking
her goddaughter's fall. Which takes the godmother's life.
Collapse. From the Latin *collapsus*: *To fall, slide. Together.*
Tiare Jones. Diana Bryant. The photograph wins a Pulitzer
Prize. Reminding us: There is beauty in the act of freefalling.
But not in the state of no-longer-falling. Then comes time
for the obbligato, for you and I to delicately say: *I turned away.*

Emmett Till, Chicago, Illinois, 1955, David Jackson

Let all the world see what I've seen, Mamie tells the photographer.

And so we bear witness with Emmett's mother, here in the back

room of the A. A. Rayner Funeral Home, gazing down—at, upon,

and through—her son. At what was done to his fourteen-year-old

body. Her eyes softly, bitterly tender. How you would want your own

abandoned body to be touched. Beside Mamie, Gene Mobley

stares directly, accusingly at us. No doubt, no confusion in his

eyes. Which say: *If you must, and you must, look upon Emmett.*

Spread out on the table. A blanket covering his ruined body. Look

at what Roy Bryant and J.W. Milan did. *When I looked at Emmett,*

I could not believe that it was even something human, Mamie will

later say. *Let all the world see.* How quickly our gaze shifts from Emmett's

swollen face to the anonymity of the shrouded body in the back.

To the comfort of an empty corked bottle. To the solace of a gold

necklace dangling from a wooden peg. Anything, anything, Emmett,

but what your unrecognizable flesh keeps telling us about us.

American Gothic (Ella Watson, U.S. Government Charwoman), Washington, D.C., 1942, Gordon Parks

As in: Handmaiden, house girl, housekeeper, housemaid, maid, maidservant, skivvy, wench. As in: Ella Watson chasing the char from the building housing the Farm Service Administration. As in: Polka dot work dress, with puffed sleeves, missing two buttons. As in: Caught between bristling broom and moping mop. As in: Every day someone must cleanse the American flag without flagging. As in Proverbs 31: *She does not eat the bread of idleness.* As in: Grant Woods created a man and a woman from Iowa oak, mother-in-law's tongue, beefsteak begonia, chiggers, ploughshare, and steeple. As in: The architecture of my face may be called gothic, but not justly my spleen. As in Grant Woods saying: *All the good ideas I've ever had came to me while I was milking a cow.* As in: If you point your camera at an American flag, expect your blood vessels to swell. As in Gordon Parks saying: *Bigots have a way of looking just like everybody else.* As in: *I picked up the camera because it was my choice of weapons. I could just as easily picked up a knife or gun.* As in: Every day someone must cleanse the American flag without flagging. As in: Stare into the eyes of Ella Watson and you will see the tiny flames contained in the word *char.*

The Burning Monk, Saigon, South Vietnam, 1963,
Malcolm Browne

You don't have to know anything about anything to bow
to this photo, states this photo. This photo refuses to self-destruct,
no matter how many times you pour gasoline on it. *The monk's*
name can be found aflame in your right palm, states this photo.
This photo wants you to extrapolate *want* from *wont*. *Meniscus*
from *umbilicus*. This photo does not care if you locate Saigon
somewhere in South Dakota. *If only you'll let me tunnel through*
your lethargy, states this photo. This photo does not care whether
you dislike or greatly dislike this photo. As it passes through your
retina, this photo devours all available light. *Warning: This photo*
is only a photo does not apply to this photo. *We have beauty. We*
have ugliness. Everybody likes beauty. But there is an ugliness,
states Weegee, offering slight comfort. *The past itself has become*
the most surreal of objects, notes Susan Sontag, offering a measure
of mercy. This photo exists inside and yet outside 1963, and,
at the same time, always at your side. This photo burns a copy
of itself inside your viscera. This photo is called *The Burning Monk*
but it could be called *Intimations of the Infinite*. This photo clings,
no matter how quickly you blink. This too you know.

GALLERY
FOUR

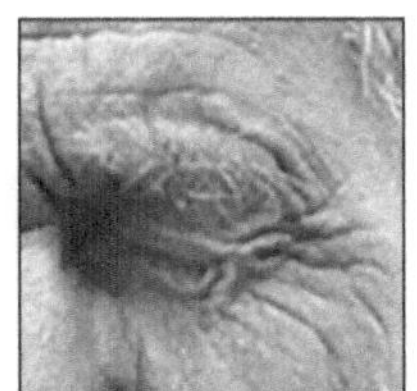

Ezra Pound, at the Home of William Carlos Williams,
Rutherford, New Jersey, June 30, 1958, Richard Avedon

What is it you so badly don't want to see, Ezra? That shuts

the eyes, shuts the eyes tight. Blotting out every everlasting

strand of light. How this lovely blindness pulls on the skin,

deepens each wrinkle, weighs your body down, as it digs in

and in. You feel it unfold your throat, falter your tongue, tug

your mouth apart, let a breath enter and wither. You hear

a hand crumpling stiff paper, a fist pulling the fibers together,

so all the inky letters merge. *Blood alone moves the wheels*

of history now a quivering wet black speck. Your eyes pulse

a marbled green-black against marbled black-green. Your eyes

shut tighter, until you see chicken wire stalls in a warehouse

where you stashed the disassembled moon, each piece

labelled in a Confucian code only you could understand.

And then forgot. Your shut eyes see the curved fragments

of the moon. They glow off, on. On, off. A hand pours

a cup of cool water over a palpitating rock. No, Ezra,

pours unarticulated water over your desiccated heart.

Pictures on Top of Phonograph, Yonemitsu Home,
Manzanar War Relocation Center, California, 1943, Ansel Adams

Relax. This could be any 1940s home. But for what the photo
won't show. *A concentration camp is a place where people
are imprisoned. Not because of any crimes they have committed.
But simply because of who they are.* Who they are: A phonograph
decorated with family items. A photo of a young Japanese American
male in uniform. He's signed the photo: *Bob.* It leans against a larger
portrait: The Sacred Heart. *I will bless*, says Jesus. The blessing
obscured. Nearby, two envelopes, addressed by a graceful hand,
propped on a large flowerpot. Letters from Bob on the battlefield.
Below his photo, papers: Kanji and four signatures. Clean lace doily
under the flowerpot. Decorated with a large ribbon. Big bow. Off
to the right, an orange and a small melon radiating geometric lines
from one end, as if painted by someone with too much time. *This*,
concludes the photo, *is the Yonemitsu family.* Surrounded by swirling
barbed wire. Shifting listless sand. Bored, boring guards with machine
guns—aimed at those within. You could say: *Did Ansel Adams arrange
the items on the phonograph?* You could say: *Manzanar means* apple
orchard *in Spanish.* You could say: *This is not an aerial surveillance
photo.* Say: *Particles of truth cling to the surface of the tongue.*

Drowned Migrants, Matamoros, Mexico, June 24, 2019,
Julia Le Duc

Two bodies, face down on a sandy bank of the Rio Grande,

a blue beer can bobbing nearby. Oscar Alberto Martínez

Ramírez and Valeria. The 23-month-old girl tucked inside

her father's black t-shirt, right arm reaching around his neck.

Oscar's wife, Tania Vanessa Ávalos, said he crossed the river

with Valeria on his back. Told to wait there, on the U.S. shore,

his daughter, seeing him swim away, to help her mother,

Valeria plunged into the river. Fighting the current, Oscar

grabbed his daughter, pulling her inside his t-shirt. But a river

god is a jealous god. Even when not jealous. Just as the gut

of the president is an angry gut. Even when not angry.

Asked about the dead migrants, Trump stated the twenty-five-

year-old Salvadoran father *probably was this wonderful guy.*

On the same day Oscar and Valeria were found, the Rio Grande

gave up four more bodies: a twenty-year-old woman, a toddler,

and two infants. *Probably all were wonderful people,*

you might say, quietly, loudly, if someone had removed

your heart, leaving in your chest a bobbing beer can.

Untitled (Woman Holding Up a Shot Glass of Rye),
Storyville, New Orleans, Louisiana, 1912, E. J. Bellocq

She contemplates the shot glass, raising it high, avoiding

our eyes. Head resting on her left arm, hair pinned up, loose

shawl arranged over one shoulder, she's dolled up for her

portrait. Her bold, striped stockings telling us she's loud,

saucy, adores a bawdy joke or two. The bottle of Raleigh rye

on the side table proudly proclaims: *Every night is party night.*

Those portraits on the wall behind her— family members who

stare with disapproval? Or faux decorations to make the customer

feel he's not in a brothel? On the shelf under the table, someone's

carefully placed handcrafted dollhouse chairs. Pressed leaves

rising from the chair backs. Did our shot-of-rye woman make them?

She'd rather you not ask her real name, her hometown. Anything

about brothers, sisters, parents. When she arrived in Storyville.

Where she'll go—after. The alarm clock says noon. Midnight,

she'll be engaged. *On stage I make love to twenty-five thousand*

people. Then I go home alone, said Janis Joplin. Tossing back

her shot of rye, the dimpled woman in the striped stockings tells

E.J. Bellocq, *You look like you could use one too, Hon.*

Old Man, Seven Photographs, Philadelphia, Pennsylvania, 1880s, Thomas Eakins

Could it be? This anonymous naked old man is our camerado

Walt Whitman? *Hankering. Gross. Mystical. Nude.*

As the old man disrobes, Eakins tells him, *A woman naked is*

the most beautiful thing there is—except a man naked.

In the first three photos, we see the subject with arms raised,

hands locked behind the head. To better let us observe his

profile, gentle arc of slender belly slightly protruding. In photos

three and four, the old man with the wispy, untamed beard—hands

folded behind his back—faces the viewer. Totally unashamed,

he lets us gaze at will, his groin in full view. By pose five, he's

even more comfortable, his stance slightly wider, left leg further

forward, weight on his right leg. He begins to recite "When I Heard

the Learn'd Astronomer," but we tell him, *Really, there's no need.*

In the last two photos, we see his back, the long furrow running

down his spine. *The poet always stands naked before the world,*

says Allen Ginsberg, at a reading of "Howl" in Los Angeles, hurling

his clothes at an all too corporeal heckler. *At last America will see me*

as I am, Whitman tells Thomas Eakins that afternoon in Philadelphia,

examining the seven photos, his body's poetry. Or is this just

some old man with a scraggly beard, hungry for a day's wage?

The Kiss at City Hall, Paris, France, April 1, 1950,
Robert Doisneau

He told us we were charming. Asked if we could kiss again.

For the camera. We didn't mind. We were used to kissing,

remembers Françoise Delbart. On kissing Jacques Corteaud,

her boyfriend, on rue de Rivoli. *I don't photograph life as it is,*

says Robert Doisneau, *but life as I would like it.* Admitting

that the famous Parisian kiss—seen on cards, postcards, posters—

was posed. Along with many other unreal kisses, on many other

avenues. The camera embracing the two aspiring actors for *Life*

magazine's *The Lovers of Paris.* But only this photo, only this kiss

became famous. Allowing us to see the physics of a kiss: Each

lover's chest turned to the other's. His right hand resting lightly

on her shoulder. Her right arm relaxed, yet slightly bent. The fingers

of his left hand coming together as if pinching a bees' wing.

Their eyes shutting out the noisy, distant world. Passersby

busy passing by. All they know of love and death—commingling

at the lips. *We were kissing all the time*, recalls Françoise.

It was delicious. Perhaps we should stop here. Nine months

after *The Kiss*, Françoise and Jacques are lovers no more.

Washing Up in a Brothel, Rue Quincampoix,
Paris, France, circa 1932, Brassaï

On the bidet, she sits, head bowed, back to the prying

camera. Nearby, draped over the sink, a white towel,

with tousled fringes. Off to the right, her customer,

in white shirt, black slacks, in a hurry to leave. Face

hidden, he pretends to tie a shoelace. His suspenders

not yet fastened. Light glances off the back of her shoe.

Off her white stocking.   Strokes her bare buttock as she

waits on the bidet for the voyeur with a camera to go

away. The curtain, pulled tight and tucked around a pipe,

declares: *No one can see in; therefore, no one can see*

out. In the framed mirror, note the decorative flower

pattern. An attempt to tell the viewer: *This too is*

beautiful. The mottled rubber hose running from sink

to bidet insists all are complicit. Even the rubber sink plug

on a chain. *The beauty of evil,* declares Brassai. Surely

he means: *The evil of banality.* For there's nothing erotic

here. *Are you through now?* calls the woman on the bidet.

Object (Fur-Lined Tea Cup, Saucer, and Spoon), 1936

Almost anything can be covered in fur, observes Pablo

Picasso at that ineluctable café in Paris where all great ideas

are spawned. Meret Oppenheim nods, staring at the Eiffel Tower,

imagining the steel girders clothed in fur. Dora Maar objects:

Fur belongs where it longs to be, on the animal it belongs on.

At that moment, André Breton, lowered by fishing line

from the ceiling, says, *Everyone wants to feed on the Marvelous.*

And then he asks the waiter for an ant dipped in brass dipped

in chocolate.   Later, Oppenheim covers a saucer, tea cup, and spoon

with fur. Chinese gazelle fur. Exhibited at the Charles Ratton

Gallery, in Paris, the *Object* causes one viewer to faint. Others

complain of headaches. Hypothermia. Amnesia. Just glancing

at a gallery photo of the *Object* may induce premature reincarnation.

In the café that day, Meret Oppenheim notices her tea has grown

cold. She tells the waiter, A *little more fur, s'il vous plait.*

Painter's Wife [Helene Abelen], Cologne, Germany, circa
1926, August Sander

Those ballooning Turkish pants. Man's white shirt. Black tie.

Cigarette in mouth. Man's haircut. And that feral look in the eye—

confident yet fearful. Meet Helene Abelen. Or Frau Peter Abelen,

as she would have been introduced in 1926. Match in hand, she's

about to combust. Note the twitching left foot. *The person is*

mobile, says the photographer. *And then I freeze one moment*

in his movement. A mere five-hundredth of a second of that person's

lifetime. Please, he tells Frau Abelen: *Hold still. I beg you.* Pleads

with her to pose for yet another, stiller, portrait for his *Face*

of Our Time collection. *A still life,* she replies, *is for inanimate*

objects. Then laughs. The photographer offers a stiff, polite smile.

Those paintings behind her—her husband's. Or is she implying

she's the *force majeure?* The Nazis do not approve. In 1936

they seize all copies of *Face of Our Time.* Burn them. Visit

the photographer' studio, destroy every plate. *I never made*

a person look bad, says August Sander. *They do that themselves.*

Steer Skull, Badlands, Pennington County, South Dakota,
August, 1936, Arthur Rothstein

What the photo lets us see: A sun-bleached skull

of a steer on dry, sun-baked earth. What the critics

of FDR and his alphabet soup of federal programs saw:

A prop moved many times. To make farming conditions

in the Dust Bowl look even worse. In other words:

Propaganda. I moved the skull, confesses Arthur Rothstein,

ten feet. For exercises in photography. To study the texture

of the skull. Cracks in the soil. How the Badland light

pitched and seethed. Say the critics: *Thou shalt not*

alter thy photograph. In any way. Ever. Amen.

The word *photograph* offering little help: *Photo.*

As in *light. Graph.* As in *to write. I write with light,*

says the camera. *To reveal unto you the terrible truth.*

Can a skull be moved, say ten feet, to write more clearly

with the light? To better illumine the sun-bleached truth?

What if everything we saw was real, yet nothing was

as it appeared? wonders the wandering skull of the steer.

Says Arthur Rothstein's boss: *That goddam skull.*

Dali Atomicus, Life Magazine, 1948, Philippe Halsman

How the angry atoms hum. Dali, brush in hand, surges up, violating

the immortal laws of gravity. His easel and unfinished canvas

likewise aloft. A tilting chair floats ominously nearby. A long

carpet of water arcs up, then gushes down, hovering over the floor.

Three black cats, one alongside the crest of water and two below, fly

by with invisible bat wings. To the right, an untethered footstool

below Dali's *Leda Atomica* floats up. In that canvas, Leda and

the swan erotically levitate. Giving birth to *Dali Atomicus.* Everything

in motion, everything at rest. 28 times the photographer and his crew

toss the three shrieking cats. 28 times they toss the sturdy bucket

of unbridled water. But something is missing. *I want to blow up*

a chicken, Dali tells Halsman, *in homage to the atomic bomb. You must*

get that in the photo too, Philippe, the exploding chicken and all

its little clucking atoms. But the atoms, says the weary photographer,

they're too exhausted to stir. And so, Dali's chicken lives. As do

its suspended eggs, soon to be plucked by the weightless hand of gravity.

*Car Accident—U.S. 66, Between Winslow and
Flagstaff, Arizona,* circa 1955, Robert Frank

It's all right. You can stare. Mr. Frank certainly is.

You can't see him and his camera, but he's here, watching

us. I don't know who spread the wool blanket over me, but

it doesn't matter. Maybe one of the four mourners lined up

behind me in the weeds. The woman hugs herself tightly,

staring down at me as if I was contagious. The man beside

her turns, telling her something she's already forgotten.

The two men in cowboy hats have nothing to say. One folds

his long arms behind him, as if he's handcuffed; the other clutches

his hands by his abdomen. You ask what's that in the dirt nearby?

Stone slabs from broken flooring. In the background,

two barren homes, an empty garage, a small shack, and

an outhouse, all disappearing into the ghostly winter hue.

I don't think there's much more to say. Mr. Frank doesn't

want you to see the mangled car, the traffic shushing by

Highway 66, or the shoes I was wearing. He only wants

you to ponder that unseen figure under a coarse blanket,

alongside a highway, in stealthily falling snow. Just that.

Bergen-Belsen, Bergen, Germany, April 19, 1945,
Photographic Department of the British Army

On they swam, far below the starless earth, for so many

nights. Shedding spittoon, phonograph, tea cup, monocle.

Shedding ottoman, chamber pot, carpet, doily. Paring butcher

block, handkerchief, colander, even the ceiling soot. Everything

that told them where they had dived, how the earth propelled

them so. On they swam, so many nights below, their bodies

pushed, their bodies pulled, until they surfaced. Naked. Pulsing,

panting. But why here? Why this faceless place? The good

townspeople can only say: *They swam, far below the starless*

earth, for so many nights. Perhaps the swimmers heard, far

below, the fiddle made from a femur. Smelled bread made

from boiling brambles. Heard a child caught in a crow's throat

call: *Come up, up from the ground.* Such an irresistible pull

must have seized them. So frail, so bony, so bruised. Panting,

pulsing. So many gasping no more. Please. Tell us why.

The good townspeople only say: *They swam. Far below*

the starless earth. For so many nights. The bodies, so many

pilfered bodies, piled one on the other. In long, aching rows.

Listening for the sound. For the child caught in the throat

to call: *Come down. Down under the ground.*

Boy Reading to Elephant, Mexico City, Mexico, 2008,
Gregory Colbert

Bound by bend and wrinkle, linger and hide, an elephant

waits, with all its weight. For centuries. The boy's measured

mouth open-shut-opens, in one flutter-motion. *To kneel is to*

lean is to listen, he reads. *To listen is to kneel is to read.*

His voice lifts the words from the page. Each page, weightless

without words, floats past The Garden of Resting Sleep. Above

The Canyon of Heavenly Remorse. Into the Saltless Sea

of Wordlessness—though pieces of words sometimes salt the sea.

On the shore, the boy gathers word scraps. He builds an elephant

with trees for legs. He builds a cottage inside the elephant, with a tiny

elephant inside a cage. He builds a gun, which fires the phrase: *I Too*

Am a Piece of the Sky. He keeps it in the broom closet, next to

the inflatable moon. Whenever he opens the broom closet door,

the gun says, *One morning I shot an elephant in my wife's nightgown.*

What I was doing in her frilly pink nightgown, I'll never know.

This is not something you would ever tell an elephant named Darling,

so the boy keeps the door to the broom closet locked, except for those

nights when he must inflate the moon. *Dearest darling,* the boy recites.

To read is to be wrought is to be read. Let us rejoice. Bend and wrinkle,

linger and hide. An elephant's still listening ignites the mutable air.

The Moon Belongs to the People!!!, Brooklyn, New York, 1971, Stephen Shames

Those who spray the word *moon* with anonymous black paint

on a faceless brick wall in a shiftless lot say the moon belongs

to the soundless vowel birthed without end. The trashed weeds

below the graffiti say the moon belongs to those who stumble,

breaking the radius, cracking the ulna. Those who know

the lunar landing was filmed in a Hollywood backlot say

the moon belongs to those whose blood can be heard whirling

and wheeling in mole and bat. Those who have seen the moon

impaled by a flag say the moon belongs to those clutching

broom, mop, spatula, potato peeler. Those who writhe about

at night with a spinal lurch say the moon belongs to the just-before-

dawn fox unleashing its disembodied all-too-human shriek.

The woman with the moon inscribed into her back says, *The moon*

pretty much belongs to no one, which is why my tongue throbs.

Those who swear they can see, without any telescope, Buzz

Aldrin's footprint immolating the moondust, say, *Can't we talk,*

for a moment, about something else? If someone were to text

the moon, in its language of granular insomnia, we all know

what it would say: *The moon has no comment on earthly*

concerns. Remember: The moon belongs only to the moon.

NOTES

Herbert Bayer's *Lonely Metropolis* is a photomontage.

"*Home of a Rebel Sharpshooter,* Devil's Den, Gettysburg, Pennsylvania, July 5, 1863, Alexander Gardner": Many believe that the body in this photo was moved by Gardner for multiple photographs. Historian William Frassanito noted this in his book *Gettysburg: A Journey in Time.*

"*Billy the Kid and the Regulators Playing Croquet,* Tunstall Ranch, Lincoln County, New Mexico, 1878, Tintype": Photographer not known.

"*Arizona War Worker Writes Her Navy Boyfriend a Thank You Note for the 'Jap' Skull He Sent Her,* May 22, 1944, Ralph Crane": The four questions Nickerson asks the skull come from *Hamlet.* The skull's quote, *In you is the presence that will be, when the stars are dead,* can be found in *The Selected Poetry of Ranier Marie Rilke,* tr. Stephen Mitchell. The editors of *Life* note about this "Picture of the Week": *The armed forces disapprove strongly of this sort of thing.*

"*Behind the Gare Saint-Lazare,* Paris, France, 1932, Henri Cartier-Bresson": Cartier-Bresson stated: *The creative act lasts but a brief moment, a lightning instant of give-and-take, just long enough for you to level the camera and to trap the fleeting prey in your little box.*

"*Spanish Wake,* Deleitosa, Spain, 1951, W. Eugene Smith": Some of the villagers identify the dead man in the photo as Juan Larraz. For more on the anger of the villagers over Smith's photos, see John Banning's "Eugene Smith's 'Spanish Village' Revisited."

"*Isadore Greenbaum Dragged Out of Madison Square Garden by Police*": Photographer not known.

"*Pile of American Bison Skulls Waiting to be Ground into Fertilizer*, Rougeville, Michigan, 1892": The Detroit Public Library website notes this is handwritten on the back of the photo: "C.D. 1892 Glueworks, office foot of 1st St., works at Rougeville, Mich." Photographer not known.

In "*Excusado*, Mexico, 1925, Edward Weston": In *Time, Myth and Erasure: Tina Modotti and Edward Weston*, author Gary Higgins describes Modotti this way: "In Modotti, Weston would find a friend, muse, apprentice, translator, agent, studio manager, and occasional porter, cook, and maid." Henry David Thoreau wrote: *It's not what you look at that matters. It's what you see.*

"*Bomb Shelter*, Garden City, New York, 1955": Photographer not known.

"*Bob Dylan at the Typewriter, The Minnesota Daily*, University of Minnesota, Minneapolis, Minnesota, 1959": Photographer not known.

"*Emmett Till*, Chicago, Illinois, 1955, David Jackson": This poem is in memory of Mamie Mobley. *Time* magazine credits David Jackson with this photo, but another photographer has also been named in the *New York Times*: *Gus Savage, editor and publisher of* The American Negro: A Magazine of Protest, *said he had been the first to print a photograph of Emmett Till's body, taken by a schoolteacher named Lester Davis before the public viewing, when the corpse was on a slab in the funeral home.*

"*Ezra Pound, at the Home of William Carlos Williams*, Rutherford, New Jersey, June 30, 1958, Richard Avedon": Benito Mussolini said: *Blood alone moves the wheels of history.*

"*Object (Fur-Lined Tea Cup, Saucer, and Spoon)*, 1936": There are various gallery photos of the *Object*, and no photographer is credited for them.

About the Author

JOHN BRADLEY was born in Brooklyn, New York, and grew up in Framingham, Massachusetts; Lincoln and Omaha, Nebraska; Massapequa and Lynbrook, New York; and Wayzata, Minnesota. He is the author of eight previous full-length books of poems, prose poems, and aphorisms and the editor of three anthologies. His first book, *Love-In-Idleness: The Poetry of Roberto Zingarello*, won the Washington Prize in 1989, and a second edition, expanded and revised, was published by Word Works. He is the recipient of two National Endowment for the Arts Fellowships, a Pushcart Prize, and grant from the Illinois Arts Council. For over twenty years he has been reviewing books of poetry for *Rain Taxi*. He lives in DeKalb, Illinois, with his wife, Jana, and their cats, Kiki and Zuzu.